LOST TALES

Adam Murphy

~for Ezra~

Lost Tales
is a
DAVID FICKLING BOOK

First published in Great Britain in 2016 by
David Fickling Books,
31 Beaumont Street,
Oxford, OX1 2NP

Text and Illustrations © Adam Murphy, 2016

978-1-910989-19-7

1 3 5 7 9 10 8 6 4 2

Papers used by David Fickling Books are from
well-managed forests and responsible sources.

FSC
www.fsc.org

MIX
Paper from
responsible sources
FSC® C017574

DAVID FICKLING BOOKS Reg. No. 8340307

A CIP catalogue record for this book is available
from the British Library.

Printed and bound in Great Britain
by Sterling.

table of contents

Strong Wind
and
Little Scabs

~an old Mi'kmaq tale~

Once upon a time, in the land of the Mi'kmaq, on America's north-east coast, there lived a great warrior named Strong Wind.

No one had ever seen him, because he was invisible, but everyone knew the tales of his heroic deeds, his great wealth, and his kindness.

It was well known that Strong Wind would marry whoever could see him.

So, one by one, all the girls in the village would go to his tent to try their luck.

There they were met by his sister, who lived with him.

She could see him, so when it was time for him to return home, she took the prospective bride down to the water...

Can you see him?

Y-yes...

All right, what's his bowstring made of?

Each girl she would ask this, or, "What does he pull his sled with?" or something similar, and always they would answer...

Uh, a piece of rawhide...?

Or...

A flexible green branch.

And then she would know that they had lied, and they couldn't really see him.

And so, one by one, all the girls in the village tried their luck... and all went home disappointed.

Now, at the other end of the village, lived an old man with three daughters.

Since he was a widower, they were left alone while he went out during the day.

And I am sorry to report that the elder ones were very cruel to the youngest.

They gave her all the hardest chores.

They cut off all her hair and allowed her to wear only rags.

And worst of all, they pushed her into the fire...

So that she was covered with burns and scabs.

"Little Scabs", they called her.

When their father came home, they said she had fallen in herself.

Man! What **makes** people act like this!? I don't know.

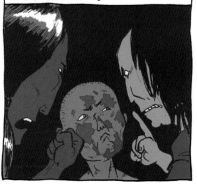

They must've been really unhappy inside, to have to try so hard to put it onto somebody else.

9

Whatever it was, they sure made life miserable for Little Scabs.

Now, of course, those two girls thought very highly of their own appearance.

So naturally they went to try their luck at winning Strong Wind.

But first the eldest...
then the middle sister, came home disappointed.

As if Strong Wind the Kind-Hearted would marry vicious young witches like those two!

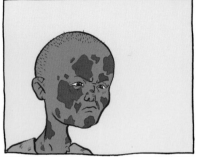

Well, one day the little one, the one they called Little Scabs, decided to take **her** chance to win the hand of Strong Wind.

She had only rags to wear, but she made a sort of dress from birch bark.

And, since she had no shoes, she borrowed a pair of her father's moccasins, which were **way** too big for her.

What the...?

Go on then! Make a fool of yourself!

As if Strong Wind would marry a little **scab** like you!

With...with... The **Spirits' Road.** *

*We call it the Milky Way.

You really **have** seen him...

SPLOT

He's crying...?

Tears of joy, my dear.

His true bride has come at last.

So, you can see me...?

Yes.

And I see you...

And so Strong Wind married Little Scabs, who no one called "Little Scabs" any more...

13

...and they all lived happily ever after in the big tent by the lake

The Gifts of Wali Dad

an old Punjabi tale

Once upon a time, in the land of **Punjab**, there lived an old grass cutter who prized **virtue** above all else. He was known by the name of **Wali Dad**.

He'd been a grass cutter all his life, which meant that he made his living by cutting long grass, bundling it up, and selling it for farmers to feed their animals.

This only paid him **three pennies** a day. But then, Wali Dad was a simple man and he lived a simple life.

Since he cared only for virtue and had no time for luxuries, his simple needs only cost him **two pennies** a day.

The extra penny he put in a big pot that he kept at the back of his little hut.

CLINK!

Well now, one day, he thought:

Maybe I should have a look at this pot...

KRSSSSH!

Saints alive! What am I going to do with all this money!?

Seriously, though... I don't have a use for it— I already have everything I need.

Could buy a new pot...

No! it should be something **really** virtuous! That's what I'm all about...

Maybe a gift...

A gift for the most **virtuous** lady in the world!

Wali Dad!

My friend!

Travelling merchant.

This is a pleasant surprise! I don't normally see you unless you've got grass to sell...

What can I do for you?

You've been all over the world, while I've always stayed here. Tell me... who is the most **virtuous** lady that you know of?

Hmm, let's see... without a doubt, that would be the **Princess of Khaistan.**

Beautiful as the Moon she is, and also wise, generous and compassionate.

Why do you want to know?

Would you be so kind, the next time you're passing...

To give her this little gift. A token of esteem from one who values virtue more than wealth.

Ha ha! Sure, Wali Dad, why not? I'd be happy to!

And so, in the throne room of Khaistan...

?

Wali Dad?

Never heard of him.

17

Send him the appropriate response, will you?

Majesty...

You should've seen her face!

I think she liked it, though...

It was a nice gesture.

Wali Dad?

The Princess of Khaistan thanks you for your gift, and sends you these fine silks in return.

HA HA HA! You've gone and done it now!

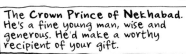

But... What on earth am I going to do with this?

HA HA HA HA HA HA

You don't happen to know anyone else who is virtuous, and could use a pile of fine silks?

HEE HEE HEE HEE

Har har. Actually, I know just the person...

The Crown Prince of Nekhabad. He's a fine young man, wise and generous. He'd make a worthy recipient of your gift.

Would you mind...

I'm just going past his palace. I'd be happy to pass it along.

But, at the Prince's palace...

Wali Dad?

Never heard of him.

That's a pretty sweet gift, though. Better send him something good in return...

Well, thanks. I'm glad **that's** sorted...

Wali Dad?

The Prince of Nekhabad thanks you for your most excellent gift, and in return sends you these finest Arabian horses.

Hoo hoo hoo! Luck's just not on your side, my friend!

What am **I** going to do with horses?

Look, I hate to be a bother...

Hee hee... No bother, but I don't really know anyone else...

But I **am** going past the Princess of Khaistan's palace again tomorrow...

Oh, thank you my friend, thank you! Please, just get them out of here!

But, at the Princess' palace...

This is getting ridiculous.

What do I do?

Majesty, if I might make a suggestion...

Send him a gift so magnificent...

so **stupendous**...

He will **never** be able to repay!

...And so he'll stop pestering me with gifts...

MWA HA HA HA

You know, that just might work...

Wow - that is **quite** a gift...

I have a feeling this is going to make Wali Dad very happy...

Well, thank goodness that's over! Nothing like the simple life...

Another gift from the princess!?

My friend, while you're travelling, would you...?

Take it to the prince!?

Is that really a good idea?

Please! **I** don't want all this stuff! What am I going to do with it all!?

At the Prince of Nekhabad's...

Who is this guy!?

I've never seen such amazing presents!!

Send him something even **more** amazing!

My lord, I don't know if we can...

What!!? **Scour** the treasury! **Sell** stuff if you have to! I'll not be outdone by **anyone** on generosity!

...

No no **NO**! I will **not** take this stuff to the princess!

This is **madness**! When will it end!?

Please! Just one more! I'll never ask for anything **ever** again! Just... **get it out of here..!**

Your majesty, it would appear that my plan has failed...

We cannot match this gift...

Wow. I think I'd better go **meet** this Wali Dad, who gives such amazing gifts.

The princess is coming here!?

Oh God! What will I do!?

I told you it would all end in disaster...

She thinks I'm some big shot, but I'm just a poor, lowly grass-cutter! Oh the shame! I'm such a fool!

HA! HA! HA! HA! HA! HA!

Just... hold the fort for me. I'll... think of something...

...

Why, why, why did I **ever** think this was a good idea!?

What an idiot! Now the **whole world** will know what a fool I am.

I should just **throw myself** off this cliff. End this whole hideous mess right now...

21

Wali Dad...

Don't worry so, Wali Dad. You may be poor, but you have the heart of a king.

Go home. God protects those who trust in him.

"God protects those who trust in him!?" That's your plan?

Why? You got a better one?

Make way for the Princess of Khaistan!

DUN DA DA DAAAAA!

Too late now...

You sure we haven't taken a wrong turn somewhere?

This should be it...

Clear the way for the Crown Prince of Nekhabad!

DUN DA DA DAAAAA!

What the...?

The prince is here as well!? You're really for it now...

Not helping...

And so the prince and the princess were married amidst great rejoicing.

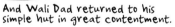

And Wali Dad returned to his simple hut in great contentment.

And though he often thought of his friends the prince and princess...

Lucky Jim
and the
Golden Hair of
the Sun

an old Romani tale

There once was a king who got lost while he was out hunting. Night was drawing in, when he came across a poor charcoal-burner's hut.

Please your majesty, I can't show you the way to the palace tonight, my wife is giving birth!

Hm. Well, I **guess** that's a decent excuse...

If you'll be good enough to take this room, I'll show you the way first thing tomorrow...

But the king couldn't get a wink of sleep on account of the wife's labour pains in the next room.

AAAAAGH!

That's right, darling... **Breathe**...

Oh, for Heaven's sake!

Until, suddenly, it was over.

...

Thank goodness!

WAAAAH!

What is going **on** in there?

OOH HOO HOO HOO!

WAAAH!

WAAAH!

OOH HOO HOO!

Whoa! What am I even looking at here?

What the king was looking at were **The Fates**, the three sisters who, since the dawn of time, have woven the destiny of every creature, great and small, in the grand tapestry of life.

Well, what do you see for **this** child, my sisters?

Oh, oh! Sorrow and woe! Not an hour old and already his mother is dead and his father is too poor to raise him.

But there is **worse** sorrow yet to come.

Sorrow, aye sister, but it is out of that sorrow that great **joy** will come...

26

Isn't that the way for **all** mortals...?

Aye, that's the way... But **what** will his great joy be, sisters?

Heh heh heh... At this **very moment**, a princess is born to the king who sleeps in the next room!

And **this boy** shall one day become her husband and inherit that kingdom!

Well, if the king slept badly before, he slept **even worse** after that.

A filthy peasant! Marry my daughter? Inherit my kingdom!? Not ruddy likely!

And so, the next morning...

That way to the palace, your majesty...

Would that I might find my **own** way so easily...

It occurs to me that you are distressed because your wife is dead and you don't think you can support your son by yourself...

Yes, I know, you are amazed at my insight.

But I say this not to demonstrate my common touch, but to make you a proposal...

Give **me** the child. I will raise him as my own.

My Lord. He's all I have.

Get real, man! You **can't** raise him by yourself, out here in the middle of nowhere!

Trust me. He will never want for anything **ever again**...

And who knows? Maybe one day he will inherit my kingdom...

But the wicked king had something **else** planned for the little boy. Oh yes, my dearies, my darlings! Something else entirely!

27

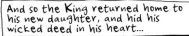

No kingdom for **you**, kid! Har har!

WAAAAAAAH!

And so the King returned home to his new daughter, and hid his wicked deed in his heart...

Until one day, years later, he was inspecting his kingdom (he was thorough like that), and happened upon a camp of gypsies.

...so you still owe me your caravan tax, and then there's...

♪

That's the horses fed, Father!

Sh! Mind your manners, son! Come and pay your respects to his majesty!

Sire.

Hm. A fine son you have, my man...

...I can't help noticing that he looks **nothing** like you or your wife...

Aye, it was the strangest thing... My wife and I always wanted a child, but alas, God never favoured us...

Until one day, I was out gathering firewood in the forest.

WAAH! WAAAH!

WAAAAH! WAAH!

Imagine! Some **monster** must've thrown a little baby off that cliff! If that branch hadn't been there...

But then he's always been lucky, haven't you, son?

That's what we call him: Lucky Jim...

Indeed...

Right about now the king was doing some feverish mental calculations: if that baby had survived, he'd be the same age as this boy here.

My man! I find I have to send an urgent message to the palace. Have you someone who might take it for me?

He'll be handsomely rewarded.

Jim'll be glad to take it, won't you, boy?

Sire.

So it was that the boy they called Lucky Jim set out with a sandwich from his mum in his knapsack, and a letter from the king in his pocket.

But oh! Sorrow and woe! If he had but known the contents of that letter...

The bearer of this letter is an enemy of the state and is to be put to death immediately.

by order of The King

But he didn't know, so he just kept on walking cheerfully towards his fate.

Man, it's getting late! Maybe I can find a place to sleep around here...

Bingo! That's lucky!

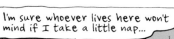

Hellooo?

Hm. Pot's still on the boil. Smells good!

I'm sure whoever lives here won't mind if I take a little nap...

But oh woe and sorrow to go! This hut belonged to a notorious **robber, thief** and **murderer**...

Z

And worst of all, he was **still at home**...

FLUSH...

And so...

Hey! What's all this!? Oh! Father!

Thank you **so much!** I was **sure** you would make me marry some awful princeling with bad breath and a rich daddy...

But instead you've somehow found **exactly** the man I've always wanted to marry! Sire, I don't know how to **begin** to thank you...

Well, that was that. The king couldn't think **how** it'd happened, but there they were; **married.** He couldn't undo it now. No thanks needed, I'm sure...

But... You **do** have the Golden Hair of the Sun, right? Sire?

Hair of the Sun. Golden. It's the traditional wedding present for marrying a princess around here. I assumed you knew...

Oh dear, oh dear. Well, you're married now, not much we can do about that. You just pop off and fetch the hair then, and we can get on with this party.

Oh oh! Sorrow and woe! And plenty of it! The new prince and princess were heartbroken to be parted so soon, but what could they do?

And poor Lucky Jim. Sorry, **Prince Lucky Jim,** hadn't the first idea even where to begin. I mean, **hair of the sun?** What even is that?

But somehow, as he wandered this way and that, his feet found their way to the shore of the great black sea at the edge of the world.

Ahoy there! Ferryman! Ahoy, young fella...

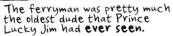

The ferryman was pretty much the oldest dude that Prince Lucky Jim had **ever seen.**

Whoa. Should you be punting that thing at your age?

Eh. It's a living.

Actually, I'm so **old**, I just want to rest in peace, but instead I just keep on living. Can't die, can't leave, I'm cursed to ferry people across this sea for eternity...

Wow. That's awful! So what's on the other side?

That's the Kingdom of the Sun. Geez, don't you even know where you're going?

The Sun leaves his castle each morning as a little baby, and comes home every night an old man.

Oh wow! That's great!

Yeah, yeah - look. Just see if you can do me a favour. The Sun sees all things that happen upon the Earth.

Maybe **he** knows how to break this curse and get free of this ferryman job, so I can finally rest in peace.

Prince Lucky Jim promised he'd do his best to find out how to help the old man. But frankly, he still didn't even know how to help himself...

Hey! What're you doing here!?

Bwah!! **Another** old person?

Yeah, I'm the Sun's grandmother.

But look, the Sun will be back any minute, and you'll be burned to a crisp! Get out of here while you can!

No, I'm sorry. I came here to fetch one of the Sun's hairs, so I can return to my princess. If that means being burned to a crisp, then so be it.

-sigh- You young folks...

All right. Hide in here and I'll see what I can do.

Also I need to know how to free the ferryman.

Fine. Fine. I'll ask about that too. Just get **in** there.

Who are you talking to, Grandmother?

No one. No one. Just talking to myself...

Now you just lie down. Get some sleep...

That's right...

OW!

PLUNK!

Ouch! Grandmother, that was **sore**!

Sorry, my dear. Sorry... I was just dreaming and I must've rolled over.

I was having the strangest dream... I saw an old ferryman who can't leave his boat, not even to die...

Oh, him? He just needs to get someone **else** to take the tiller and the curse will pass to them.

Now will you **please** let me sleep?

So now Prince Lucky Jim had his golden hair **and** his answer...

Though you may be sure he was careful not to tell the ferryman till he was safely on the other side...

You're sure you wouldn't just like a quick go?

No thank you!

And oh! Joy and rejoicing filled the palace on his return!

Even the king, though he was still far from happy with the whole thing, had to admit he was powerless in the face of Fate.

But also, he wasn't even thinking about Lucky Jim any more...

Sunbeams are actually made of **gold**!?

And that's just **one** hair...

I'll be so rich!

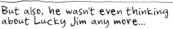

And so one day he set off, following Jim's directions until he came to the black sea.

Ferry? Oh, sorry. I'm on my break...

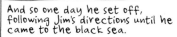

Why don't you just...

Ferry yourself...?

Two merchants

a story from the Lost Kingdom of Kanem-Bornu

Many years ago, in the long-forgotten kingdom of **Kanem-Bornu** in central Africa, two merchants were making their way home after a busy trading trip.

Now, anywhere else, you'd expect to see these guys surrounded by armed guards, for fear of bandits! But not so in the law-abiding land of **Kanem-Bornu**.

The great king, Idris Alooma, was once heard to boast that a woman could walk from one end of his kingdom to the other, covered from head to toe in **gold**, and no one would bother her!

Do I **have** to? This stuff weighs a ton!

Although, as you may have noticed, the two merchants of our tale were not equally weighed down with riches.

One had done well at the market, but he had blown all his profits immediately on wine, women and wild parties.

And now had nothing to show for it but some hazy memories and a pounding headache.

But the other merchant had saved his profits wisely, and invested in all sorts of interesting and exotic goods to sell when he got home.

And so, I am sorry to report, in the mind of the first merchant a very clever, very sneaky, very un-Kanem-Bornian plan began to form...

My friend, you must be exhausted, carrying all that stuff. Let me take your bag for you, at least until we get to the next town...

That's very kind of you.

Not at all!

Least I can do...

The next town was the great capital city, **N'gazargamu**.

Well, thanks again, friend.

I'll take my stuff back now...

Your stuff? What are you talking about...?

Oh, no way! He wasn't being nice— it was a trick all along!

Now, no one prized truth, fairness and honesty more highly than the good people of Kanem-Bornu.

But alas, it can be hard to tell the difference between an honest attempt to recover stolen property and a common brawl.

And so our two merchants found themselves visiting the palace of the great king, Idris Alooma.

Your majesty, we arrested these two brawling in the street...

You know, if there's one thing I can't stand, it's people brawling in my streets...

Your majesty! He took all my stuff and now he won't give it back!

Well, if there's another thing I can't stand, it's people taking other people's stuff.

But then again, we'd better hear his side of it.

One thing I really can't stand is only hearing one side of a story...

Uh oh! Is it just me, or does our sneaky merchant look like he has more tricks up his sleeve...

Your majesty! This man speaks **sign language!**

Oh good! So I can find out what he's saying.

If there's one thing I really just can't **stand**, it's not knowing what guys are saying.

Well? Go on then...

Say something.

Your majesty, I...

I can't tell you what he said...

You just said you could!

No, I mean I can't **repeat** it.

Your majesty would never forgive me...

Speak on without fear. After all, you're just the translator...

Well, your majesty. He says your mother is so ugly—

I NEVER SAID THAT!

And so, at least, justice was restored...

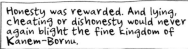

Honesty was rewarded. And lying, cheating or dishonesty would never again blight the fine kingdom of Kanem-Bornu.

Well, almost never...

Your majesty, this one says you have a huge bottom...

39

The Picture Wife

a story from Japan

Once, in the Japan of long ago, there lived a poor but hard-working peach farmer.

Now, he wasn't especially good-looking, or rich, or even all that smart, so when the most beautiful girl in the whole village agreed to be his wife, he couldn't believe his luck.

But I mean, he **really** couldn't believe it. He kept running home to check.

Wife! Wife! Are you still here!?

I'm here. Where else would I be?

I just...

...wanted to make sure...

I'm **here**. Don't worry.

OK. Sorry.

Wife! Wife!

I'm **here**. I'm not going anywhere. But shouldn't you be out in the orchard?

Those peaches won't pick themselves...

Wife! Wife!

I'm **here**.

Geez.

42

You **have** to stop doing this. We're going to go **hungry** if we don't have any peaches to sell.

I know. I'm sorry. I just... when you're not there, I start to think maybe this is all a dream... there's **no way** such an amazing woman could be my wife...

Husband. I **love** you. You're a good man.

Even if you are a bit simple.

But I think I have an idea that might help...

And so the next day, she went into town, and returned with an interesting-looking package...

There!

Fwwwp!

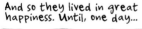
See, it says "For my darling husband". So you can stick it up while you're working, and it's just like I'm here with you.

Wife, that's **brilliant**! You're a genius!

I know...

What did I ever do to deserve you?

You're doing it right now...

And so they lived in great happiness. Until, one day...

Wife! Wife!

What's the matter?

Your...

P...picture...

It...

Blew away!

43

Well, get out there and **find** her! I **must** make her mine!

Your majesty, it says here, "For my darling husband." I think she's already married...

Don't **argue** with me, you twit! I'm the king! Do as I say!

Hmph! Must be nice to be king.

Stop complaining. What choice do we have?

See!? This is why we need a constitutional democracy...

Oh dear! Once again, fate seems to be against our happy couple...

Hither and yon roamed the soldiers of the king, searching everywhere for the lady in the picture.

Until, slowly, inexorably, they tracked her down...

EEEEEEE!

Wife?

Wife! Wife!

45

Distraught, the poor peach farmer searched everywhere for his missing wife...

Far and wide he travelled, hunting high and low for even a hint of her whereabouts...

But alas, she was nowhere to be found...

Until, having almost lost hope of ever seeing her again, he came to the great market outside the king's palace...

But, inside the palace at that very moment...

I just don't **get** it!

Ever since you came here, I've **showered** you with gifts!

Fine food, jewellery, beautiful clothes... stuff I'd have thought most girls would **kill** for!

But I haven't seen you even **once** crack a smile, let alone laugh like you did in that picture!

Bah! I just don't understand women!

Evidently, sire...

46

You think I'm a nice guy, right...?

BWA HA HA!

Wha... What is it!?

Ha Ha! That peach seller!

Hoo Hoo Hoo! He's just so **funny!**

He is?

I mean; He **is!** Very funny...

Hi! You!

Yes, you! Peach seller! Come up here!

Um...

No peasants allowed.

Hey! It's OK! Let him up!

And so our poor peach farmer entered the palace of the king...

...and he ruled wisely and well for many years...

thanks to his beautiful and clever wife

Why the Sea moans

~a story from Brazil~

So, you know that noise the waves make by the seaside, a sort of soft, moaning sss, sssss. Well, this story is from a time so long, long ago, that that noise hadn't started yet, and the sea was **totally silent**.

...

Now, in that far-off time, in a far-away kingdom, there lived a beautiful little princess named **Dionysia**.

Princess Dionysia lived in a palace **so beautiful**, it had to be seen to be believed.

Its lush, ornate gardens were filled with tropical flowers, exotic birds and sparkling fountains.

And the whole thing backed onto an enormous beach of white, silent, shining sand.

But neither the beach, nor the gardens, nor the palace, could do anything to ease the terrible **loneliness** of the poor princess.

Whenever she looked out the windows of the palace, she could see the children running and playing in the streets outside.

But, because she was a princess, she was never allowed to join in any of their games.

She was so lonely, she often went down to the sea and watched the soundless waves. So crazy lonely was she, it sometimes seemed as if the waves were calling her name: Di-on-yss-ia, Di-o-n-ysss-ia...

Di-on-ysssss-ia...

Hey, wait a minute...

Hello.

My name is Labisemena.

Would you like to be friends?

And so the princess and the sea monster became best friends.

Every day the princess would go down to the beach and they would play together from dawn till dusk.

Many years passed, and Princess Dionysia grew into a young woman.

Until, one day, Labisemena said...

Um, my dear... it's time for me to go away...

Labisemena! No!

It's OK. You're just old enough that you don't need me around any more...

But don't worry. I'm still here for you. You ever need me, just call and I'll be there.

Now it just so happened that, about this time, there lived an old king whose queen had just died.

On her deathbed, she made him promise that he would only remarry a bride whose finger fit her wedding ring perfectly.

Which seems like a funny thing to worry about when you're on the verge of death, but hey, no doubt she had her reasons...

So, once a suitable mourning period had passed, the king began sending the ring out to all the eligible princesses in the area.

And surprise surprise, guess whose finger fit perfectly?

53

But father, he's so **old**...

And so **ugly**...

Look at his **teeth**! Look at his **nails**! Ugh! There's no way I'm **kissing** that guy!

Plus, the whole setup's just **gross**. I wanna marry for **love**, not because my finger's the same size as some **dead chick's**!

Watch your tongue, girl! This guy's the **richest** king around and you're marrying him! End of story!

Geez. What is it with some people and **money**? I mean, come **on**!

The poor princess cried and cried. But no one listened. No one cared.

Have you heard!?

Just imagine! All that money!

So ungrateful!

But then she remembered that she still had **one** friend who might listen...

Labisemena!

Labisemena!

LABISEM...

OK, OK. I'm here.

Geez Louise, girl. Where'd you learn to make a noise like that?

But there's this old king, and... and...

Be cool. Be cool. I got this. Just go back. Make nice, like you're totally **OK** with everything, and then say...

I'll marry you, but only on one condition: that I have a dress the colour of the sky, the stars, and the **whole universe**.

Ha! Take that, Old King! How can such a thing even exist!?

But, far from being upset, the old king was rather pleased to have a chance to prove his "love" the only way he could... with lots and lots of **money**...

He sent his soldiers out to gather the seven greatest **dressmakers** in the whole world.

For many months they laboured, designing and cutting and sewing as if their very **lives** depended on it!

Which actually they did, because the king had promised to **execute** them all if they failed.

And so it was that fear and skill and vast wealth created a dress like nothing the world had **ever seen**...

State-of-the-art, ultra-high-tech **embroidery science** allowed the dressmakers to decorate it with whole galaxies...

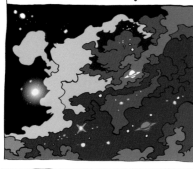

And, within those galaxies, realistically detailed exo-planets...

Each one complete with its own alien geography, eco-systems and complex societies.

Whoa.

Wearing this dress you'll be as grand, as mysterious, as **transcendentally radiant** as all **creation**!

Hooboy...

55

Ooh hoo hoo! I don't **wanna** marry the king! He's **super** old and **super** ugly!

I wanna find **love**! I wanna run **free**!

Hey, relax, will ya?

Did I not tell you; Labisemena has this **under control.**

Now, d'you bring the dress like I told you?

Sniff. Right here...

OK, cool. Now, check this out...

BRRRMMM MMMM

BLOOOP!

Whoa.

What **is** it?

It's a ship, silly. A **magical** ship.

It will take you far, far across the sea to the distant kingdom of the Handsomest Prince in **the World.**

Seriously. He's a stone **fox.** Plus he's actually a lovely guy; kind to animals, tips well, calls his mum. That sort of thing.

Anyway, he's perfect for you. So all you need to do is show up, wear your dress, marry him, and you'll be set.

Oh, Labisemena!

You're the best friend anyone could ever have! How can I **ever** repay you!?

Well, since you mention it...

Panel 1: You may not know this about me, but I'm not **actually** a sea monster...

Panel 2: Like you, I'm really a beautiful princess, but I was **cursed** with a terrible enchantment.

Panel 3: Forced to roam the seas in the disguise of a hideous monster until the curse can be broken.

Uh... Hey, guys...

Panel 4: How!? How can the curse be broken!?

Ah. Now, pay attention here...

Panel 5: The curse can only be broken by the **happiest** girl in the world, at the moment of her **greatest** happiness.

Panel 6: That'll be **you**, when you marry that prince.

Seriously. He's that good. I'd marry him myself but, well, y'now...

Sea monster...

Panel 7: All you need to do is call my name three times, at just that moment, and the curse will be broken.

All right! I'll do it!

Panel 8: Great. I knew I could count on you.

Don't forget now, y'hear?

PINKY SWEAR!

Panel 9: And so Princess Dionysia sailed away, far away...

Panel 10: Until she came at last to the kingdom of the Handsomest Prince in the World...

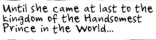

Panel 11: Pthoo!

Panel 12: OK. That must be the prince's castle...

PRINCE'S CASTLE

"OK, Princess," thought the princess. "You only get one shot. Don't go bumbling in half-cocked."

So things just kind of **stalled** for a while. As they often do in life (although not so often in fairytales...) Until, one day...

Like time-to-break-out-the-universe's-most-amazing-dress real. The prince saw her and... **BAM!** Love at first sight.

But the princess knew it's one thing to fall in love in the heat of the night, and quite another in the cold light of dawn.

"Gotta play it cool. And, y'know, eat." So she took a job in the Palace kitchen looking after the **hens**.

Palace. Ball. **Tonight.**

They danced all night to the sweet sounds of the **Samba**. (The prince was, of course, a totally awesome dancer.)

Thanks for the ring...

Wait! Come back!

Who **are** you...?

It wasn't a super-glamorous job, but it kept her fed, and it meant she could suss out the situation.

"OK, it is **on**," thought Princess Dionysia. "Situation just got **real**."

And the prince, having fallen head over heels in love with the beautiful stranger, pledged her his **ring**...

Oh. **My. God!** Have you heard!? The prince totally danced all night with some **mysterious stranger**, and now they're saying he's so obsessed with her, he won't eat or sleep!

"Come on, Your majesty. Just one bite..."

"Mmm! Smells delicious..."

"It's no use. At this rate he'll starve to death!"

"Here – allow me. This soup is so delicious, it'll snap him right out of it."

"Hey. Wasn't that her?"

"No no, your majesty. That's just the girl that tends the hens..."

"Really, are you sure? It looks a lot like her..."

"No, no. Just drink the soup. Forget about the girl. She's just a commoner..."

"Oh, don't be such an..."

AAAARRGH!

The ring! (Which you'll remember the prince had given to Dionysia the night before...)

And so (once he recovered from his soup-inflicted burns), the prince and princess were married.

And at last, after so much heart-ache, the lonely Princess Dionysia was blissfully, completely happy.

So monstrously happy, in fact, that she just completely forgot her promise to the sea monster Labisemena.

Who waited in vain for the magic that would break the evil spell.

And so that is why, if you listen very carefully to the sound of the waves, you can still hear her voice moaning...

Di-on-yssSS-ia...
Di-on-y-sssSSSS-ia...

59

The Snow Daughter

a story from Russia

Once, in far-away Russia, there lived a poor old couple.

Even though they were so poor, and so old, they were still very in love, and they would have been very happy, but for one thing...

They had no children.

Every day the old woman would sit at the window as she sewed and knitted and darned the old man's socks...

And she would watch the children laughing and playing on the village green, and it felt as though her heart would break.

And every day the old man would watch his wife as she gazed out of that window...

And he knew what she was thinking. And it felt as though **his** heart would break.

It had been this way for many years. And now, of course, they were too old to have children.

But somehow, in her heart, the old woman had never quite given up hope.

And so one day, when the snow was lying thick and still outside, she said to her husband:

Husband, let's go out and build a little snow-girl. A little snow-daughter all of our very own.

My wife. Are you sure that's a good idea?

You'll just upset yourself...

No, come on. I want to do it.

We can make her little snow eyes and snow hair and snow clothes and snow boots.

And maybe, if we love her very, very much, she might just come to life.

You never know...

So they went out into the garden, and together they made a little snow girl...

They made her snow eyes and snow hair and snow clothes and snow boots.

Oh, husband...

She's perfect.

Goodnight, little snow daughter.

Well? Go on...

Goodnight, little snow daughter.

And so the old people went to bed that night, very sad and very happy.

But in the night, something strange happened...

Something magical.

Wake up, husband.

Zzz.

Wha-whazzat?

Mother. Father. Here I am.

Born of ice and wind and rain.

Alive because you loved me so.

Little daughter of the snow.

Hello, mother. Hello, father.

I can't believe it!

Our own little girl!

Our wishes actually came true!

Mmmthr...

Ffthr...

Yr... squshing mmn...

And so it was that the little snow girl came to live with the old couple. And if only things could have stayed like that, they would have been happy forever...

Now, every day, the little snow girl would go out and play with the other children in the village.

The old people were so happy they felt as if their hearts would burst.

Look at her go!

She is our own. Our little white dove.

Until, one day, the children had all gone to play at explorers in the forest...

Hey, uh, you guys...

It's getting near teatime, and we've already come quite far...

So, uh, yeah...

But the little snow girl wasn't **ready** to go home.

Pff. **Real explorers** don't turn back because it's **teatime!**

I'm gonna see what's over that hill...

So the brave little snow girl carried on, deeper and deeper into the forest.

But it really was getting late, and before long she too was ready to go home. Which was when she realised that she didn't know which way home was!

She tried climbing a tree, but all she could see was forest in all directions.

So now she really was frightened. She had no idea how to get home, and no one knew where she was. She could be out here **forever.**

Hey, little girl. Don't cry. I'll get you home - just follow me!

65

Meanwhile, back at the village...

Ooo hoo ho! Our poor little girl! She could be frozen to **death** by morning!

Well, probably not frozen, anyway...

She is made of snow...

OK, then: **starved!** Or eaten by wolves and bears!

But, just at that moment...

Oh, thank you, Mr Fox! You **must** come and meet my parents - I'm sure they will want to repay your kindness...

Mother! Father! Don't cry! Here I am!

OK, OK, guys! Geez!

This kind fox showed me the way home.

Oh thankyouthankyouthankyou! How can we **ever** repay you!?

Here; I know. How about a nice crust of bread...?

Thank you ma'am, but I'd rather have a nice fat **hen**.

A hen!?

Well, well...

OK, then. You just wait here - let me see what I can do...

Alas! How easy it is to yearn for things we don't have, and to take for granted the things we do...

Husband. We've got our little girl back....

God be praised.

66

But, well, it seems a shame to waste a good fat hen.

I was going to make a chicken pie...

And so, I am sorry to say, the old people came up with a plan for repaying the fox's kindness...

They gave the fox a sack with a "hen" in it...

Only when he got it home he found that it wasn't really a hen at all..

That was well done, wife.

A chicken!? The nerve!

As if we were **made** of money! Especially now; we have our little white dove to think of...

But when they came back indoors, they couldn't find the snow girl any where.

You see, she knew what they had done. And so, when they came to the window...

♫ Mother, Father. Now I know. ♫

♫ Less you love me than a hen. ♫

♫ Back into the world I go. ♫

Riben, Robin and Donald McDonald

a story from Scotland

A long time ago, among the green glens and majestic mountains of sunny Scotland, there lived a poor, simple farmer by the name of Donald McDonald.

Now, although his farm was little more that a bare, rocky strip of land, with only one skinny cow, Donald was a pretty happy guy.

Or, well, he would have been, if it wasn't for his neighbours, Riben and Robin, who occupied the two massive, enormously wealthy farms on either side of him.

No matter how rich they got, it wasn't enough for them. They particularly wanted Donald's poor little strip of land, and were always plotting how to get him off it.

Pff! Look at him! With his raggedy little farm.

Bringing down the property values, he is...

And his scraggly little cow.

Disgraceful!

If something were to **happen** to that cow...

He'd be ruined! He'd have to move away.

Are you thinking what I'm thinking?

If you're thinking we should **kill his cow**, then **yes**!

And so, I am sorry to say, that is exactly what they did.

Donald found poor Daisy the next morning...

Now, faced with such terrible misfortune, most people would just go to pieces. But, sitting there on his barn floor, Donald discovered something very **strange** about misfortune...

It put **ideas** into his head. Strange, unfamiliar, **clever** ideas...

He gathered up his last few copper coins and shoved them in the cow's mouth...

Well, I'm sorry about this Daisy, but I don't expect it'll bother you, since you're dead.

And then, armed with this rather unusual fashion accessory (and a stout stick), he set off for the town tavern.

Barkeep! A pint of your finest ale, please!

WHAP!

Oh, yeah? And what will you pay me with, Donald? Everyone knows you're skint.

And kindly take that off my bar...

Pay you? Why, it's my **magic cow head** here that's paying. Just watch...

THWACK!

Hey buddy. That -er- magic cow-head of yours...

You're not looking to **sell** it, are you?

Sell it!? The **priceless heirloom** of the McDonalds, **passed down** father to son all the way back to my great-great-great grand-uncle once removed, the Black Mage of Morrar, Archibald McDonald **himself**!?

Sell a priceless source of wealth **beyond measure**, which produces a neverending fortune without end, a treasure that not even an **idiot** would part with at any **price**!?

Why, how much did you have in mind?

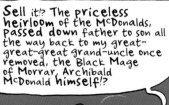

What is **wrong** with these two!? I mean **seriously**, have they no moral compass of **any sort**?

Apparently not.

Look at 'em! Just murdered an old lady and they're not even feeling guilty. What a revolting pair of human specimens.

Now, I think I already told you about Donald and misfortune – how terrible things that would have anyone else **paralysed** with grief seemed to make his brain work **overtime**.

Well, right now his brain was going a million miles an hour, and coming up with some **very** weird plans indeed...

Well, Mother, I don't think you'll like this too much. But then again you won't mind, 'cos you're dead.

Home of the richest man in town.

Son of the richest man in town.

Hey, kid – would you do me a quick favour? See that old lady over there?

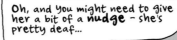

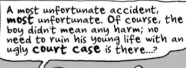

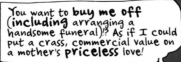

Guess what? The amazing stories you've read in this book originally appeared in...

The Phoenix
The Weekly Story Comic

The Phoenix is packed full of incredible stories, epic puzzles and non-fiction!

You can get it delivered straight to your door **every week!**

Read a free sample at
www.thephoenixcomic.co.uk/presents